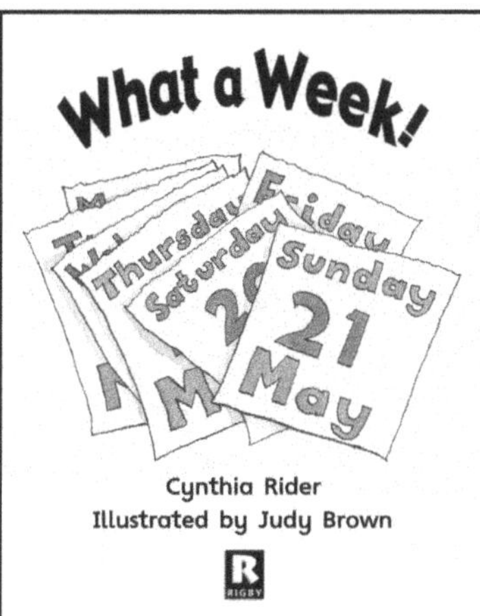

Walkthrough

This is Aunt Ann. She's in hospital.

Have you ever visited anyone in hospital?

Let's read the title together.

Talk about the meaning of 'What a Week!'

Walkthrough

Let's read the blurb together.

Can you guess the day Aunt Ann comes home?

Walkthrough

Read the title again.

What can you see in the picture?

Name the days of the week.

Do you think it's been a good week or a bad week?

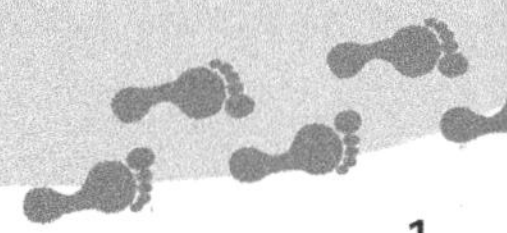

Walkthrough

This is Monday.

What do you think has happened?

Where is Aunt Ann going?

How do the little girl and her mother feel?

 ## Observe and Prompt

Word Recognition

- If the children have difficulty with the word 'Monday', model the reading of this word for them.

- Check the children can read the adjacent sounds at the end of 'Aunt'. Help them with the initial vowel sound if necessary.

- Can the children read 'hospital' using their decoding skills? If they have difficulty, model the reading of this word for them, emphasising the three syllables.

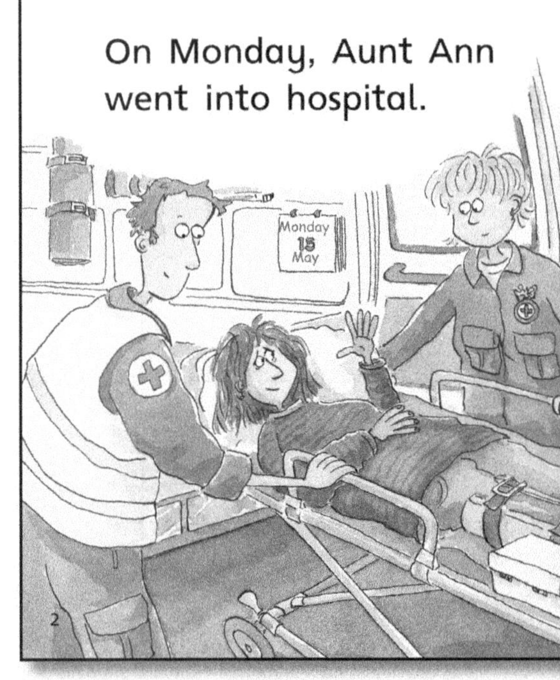

Observe and Prompt

Language Comprehension

- Check the children understand what is happening. Where is Aunt Ann going?

- How do the children think the girl and her Mum feel?

 **Observe and Prompt**

Word Recognition

- If the children have difficulty with the word 'Tuesday', model the reading of this word for them.

- Check the children can read 'visit' using their decoding skills.

- Check the children can read the word 'plant' using their decoding skills. Check they can read the adjacent consonants in this word.

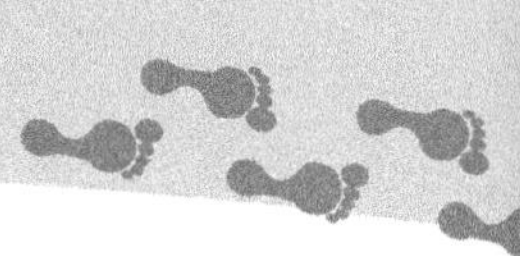

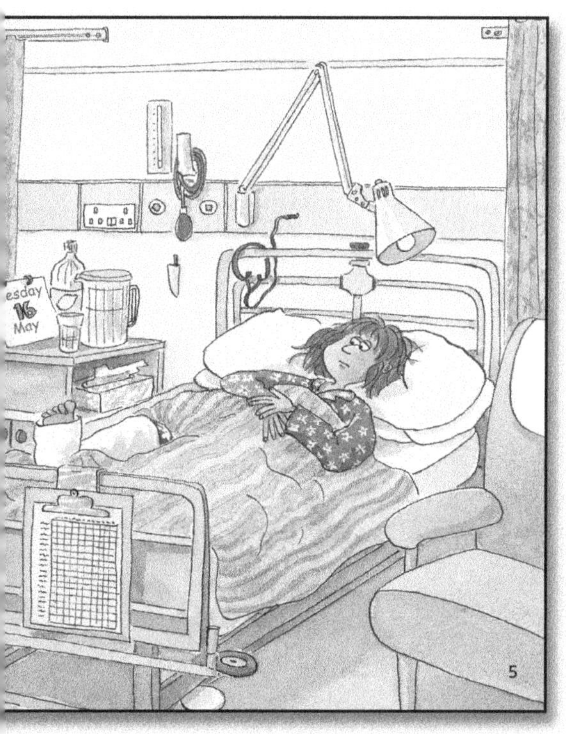

 Observe and Prompt

Language Comprehension

- Ask the children what happened on Tuesday.

- Ask the children what Mum gave Aunt Ann.

- How do the children think Aunt Ann feels?

 **Observe and Prompt**

Word Recognition

- If the children have difficulty with the word 'Wednesday', model the reading of this word.

- Check the children are reading the CVCC 'went' using their decoding skills.

- Check the children can read the word 'gave'. They may need help with the long 'a' sound (from 'a' and silent 'e').

- Check the children are reading 'book' using their decoding skills.

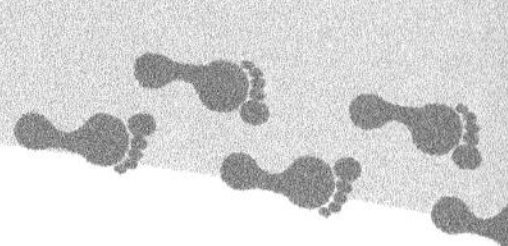

Observe and Prompt

Language Comprehension

- Ask the children what happened on Wednesday.

- Do the children think Aunt Ann liked the book?

- Who do the children think will go to see Aunt Ann on Thursday?

Walkthrough

What day is it?

This is Gran.

What has she brought for Aunt Ann?

 **Observe and Prompt**

Word Recognition

- If the children have difficulty with the word 'Thursday', ask them if they recognise the initial letters and sound – 'th', then model the reading of the word for them.

- Check the children are using their decoding skills to read the CCVC word 'Gran'. Check they can read the adjacent consonants at the beginning of the word.

- Check the children can read the word 'sweets' using their decoding skills. Can they blend the sounds through the word?

8

Observe and Prompt

Language Comprehension

- Ask the children what day it is now.

- Ask the children who came to see Aunt Ann on Thursday. What did Gran give her?

- How do the children think Aunt Ann feels today?

- Who else do the children think will come to visit Aunt Ann?

 **Observe and Prompt**

Word Recognition

- If the children have difficulty with the word 'Friday', prompt them to break it down into two syllables – 'Fri' and 'day', before blending the whole word together.

- Check the children can read 'Grandpa'. Can they say how many syllables this word has?

- Check the children can read the word 'fruit' using their decoding skills. If the children have difficulty, model the reading of this word.

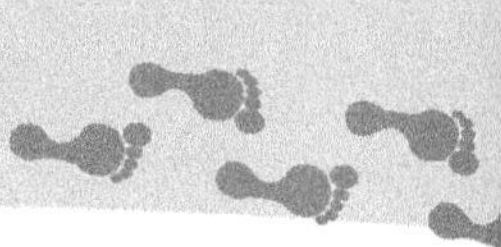

Observe and Prompt

Language Comprehension

- Ask the children who went to visit Aunt Ann on Friday.

- Ask the children what Grandpa gave Aunt Ann.

- How do the children think Aunt Ann feels today? How can they tell?

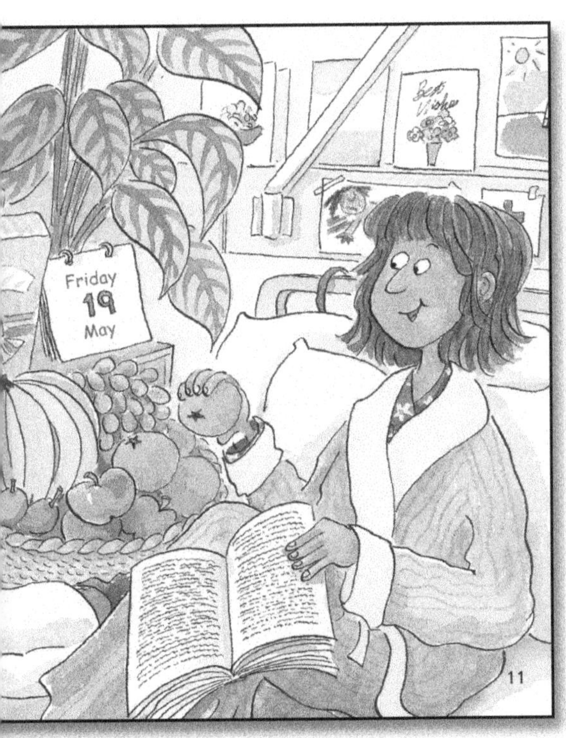

Walkthrough

Let's count from Monday to find out which day this is.

Who is visiting Aunt Ann today?

What have they brought Aunt Ann?

Is Aunt Ann feeling well?

 **Observe and Prompt**

Word Recognition

- If the children have difficulty with the word 'Saturday', ask them to break the word down into three syllables – 'Sat', 'ur' and 'day', before blending the whole word together.

- Check the children can read the sight word 'we'.

- Check the children read using their decoding skills to read 'flowers'. Check they can read the adjacent consonants in this word. Help them with the 'ow' sound if they struggle.

Language Comprehension

- Check the children understand who went to visit Aunt Ann on Saturday.

- Do the children think Aunt Ann is better? How can they tell?

- What do the children think will happen on Sunday?

What day is it today?

How long has Aunt Alice been in hospital?
(*prompt seven days, or a week, if necessary*)

What is happening on these two pages?

 ## Observe and Prompt

Word Recognition

- If the children have difficulty with the word 'Sunday', ask them to break it into two syllables – 'Sun' and 'day', before blending the whole word together.

- Check the children can read 'home' using their decoding skills. If they have difficulty, model the reading of this word for them.

- Check the children can read 'with' using their decoding skills.

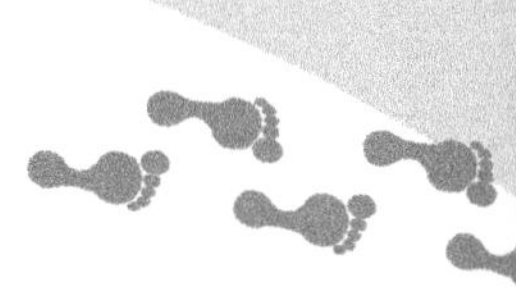

She came home with us.

15

Language Comprehension

- Prompt for expressive reading.

- Ask the children what happened on Sunday.

- Do the children think Aunt Ann is pleased to be going home? How do the family feel?

Walkthrough

What's happening here?

What do you think the little girl and Aunt Ann say?

 **Observe and Prompt**

Word Recognition

- Check the children can read 'what' using their decoding skills. If they have difficulty, ask them if they recognise the initial letters and sound – 'wh' and then to blend the word from left to right.

- Check the children can read 'week' using their decoding skills.

 **Observe and Prompt**

Language Comprehension

- Prompt for expressive reading.

- How do the children think the family feel now?

How to Use this Book

Firstly, check the learning objectives for this text (found on the back cover).

Guided Reading has three stages:

Before **Guided Reading**

Walkthrough

Take the children through the book, encouraging them to talk about the pictures and follow the events of the story. Engage them in the story by asking the questions in the band across the top of each page.

During **Guided Reading**

Observe and Prompt

As the children read the story independently, observe their reading behaviour and encourage them to use their phonic skills and knowledge as they tackle challenges in the text. Check that they are following and understanding the story by asking questions and inviting comments.

Phonic Opportunities

There are specific suggestions for embedding and checking phonic skills and knowledge. This book provides opportunities to focus on sounding out and blending phonemes to read a range of CVC words and words with final consonant digraphs.

After **Guided Reading**

Revisit and Respond

At the back of this book is a list of activities designed to develop the children's response to the story and to reinforce the teaching focus of this book.

Walkthrough

Let's look at the front cover. This story is about a troll. Who knows what a troll is?

Model the blending of 't-r-o-ll'. Ask the children to point to the word.

What is the troll wearing? What is he going to do?

Phonic Opportunity

Point to the word 'Troll'. Point to the 'T' and the final phoneme 'll'. Explain that the double 'l' makes one sound (phoneme).

Walkthrough

Let's look at the back cover. The blurb says: 'What happens to the Troll?'

Ask for and discuss suggestions.

Phonic Opportunity

Can you see anything in the picture which rhymes with 'mill'? (hill).